FRONTIERS OF THE SELLING MIND

DANIEL MCMEANS

"Frontiers of the Selling Mind," by Daniel McMeans ISBN 978-1-63868-228-8.

Published 2025 by Virtualbookworm.com Publishing, P.O. Box 9949, College Station, TX 77842, US. Copyright ©2025, Daniel McMeans. All rights reserved. No part of this publication may be reproduced, stored in a retrieval system, or transmitted in any form or by any means, electronic, mechanical, recording or otherwise without the prior written permission of Daniel McMeans.

I would like to dedicate this book to my former company, which hired me when I was 24 years old, and the management team who helped guide me as I grew into a man with many life lessons along the way to help my growth on my journey into my golden years

Right Attitude

"If you're not the lead dog, the view never changes".

Lewis Grizzard

The above quote always worked for me because it was meaningful. It's a metaphor, meaning which person do you want to be? I personally would prefer to lay my eyes on new scenery each day with new provocative thoughts and challenging the status quo. Whether I was or not didn't matter, it was the principle. If this is going to work for you, then you need to embrace a life of growth and broader horizons. I encourage you to shift your mind to performance so that you will revel at the idea of always seeing fresh, new landscapes as they always unravel.

Individualism

It's so vital that we approach our clients from a level of individuality to let your genuine, authentic persona shine in everything you do. This will be the cornerstone upon which everything is built. It's like the frame of a car, except it would be your bones. From this juncture, you will apply all your learnings, teachings, and knowledge by way of trial and error. The benefits of individuality include enhanced self-confidence, increased creativity and innovation, as well as a greater sense of purpose and fulfillment. Embracing uniqueness allows individuals to express their true selves, leading to personal growth, and self-acceptance.

"If your actions inspire others to dream to dream more, learn more, do more, and become more, you are a leader".
James Quincey (CEO of Coca Cola)

Category Specialist

The key to success in whatever business endeavor you choose is to become the master of that category. This requires a great deal of dedication, but the dividends are huge. Not to mention the respect you will gain from your clients because once they view you as an expert in your field, they will depend on you for advice and guidance. Once you have this kind of attention from your clients, that is when your business relationship soars. How do you become a master or a specialist in your category? Pick a trade journal in your field, subscribe to it, and read as much of the content as possible. Read company sponsored literature, as well. The objective is to assimilate what you have learned into a fluid speech for effective delivery and impact for your client.

One of the laws of the universe is that whatever you invest in, will return to you many times over, depending on how hard you work on it. If you fuel this law with believing in hope, the outcome can be tremendous. Why does believing in hope significantly change the outcome? When you believe in hope and in the impossible, you're tapping into a source of energy that is inexhaustible. When you combine that with being a category specialist and working hard, it all comes together, helping you create a symbiotic circle where everything is interconnected, propelling you forward to greater success.

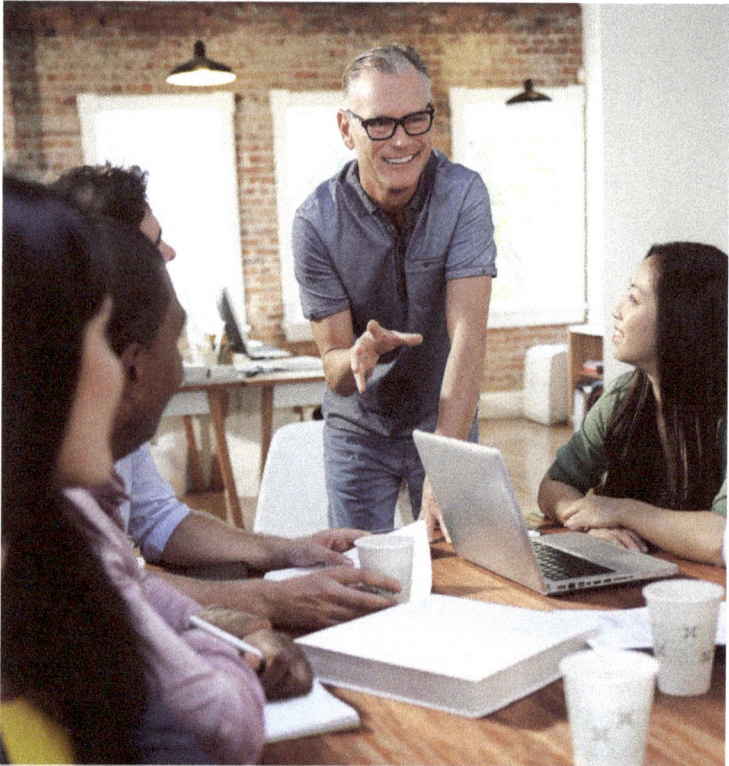

"Advances in technology, like AI and machine learning, can increase the pace of innovation even more dramatically. It's exciting to think what the future could hold"
Chris Boerner (CEO of Bristol Myers Squibb)

Know your Strengths and Weaknesses

As you advance in your sales career as a category specialist, it is essential to take stock of yourself, and your own strengths and weaknesses. This is important for several reasons. You should always be aware of your strengths and weaknesses because your strengths are what you will rely on to propel you forward with your objectives. In the back of your mind, be aware of your weaknesses, so you can continuously improve upon them. Because the way I look at it, you're always on a journey of self-improvement. As Bob Casey, the founder of United Parcel Services (UPS) said, "Success is the sum of little things done well."

Old versus New Selling Tactics

In today's fast-paced, information-driven world, the art of selling has undergone a profound transformation. The outdated "old selling" model, characterized by aggressive tactics and a transactional focus, has given way to a sophisticated "new selling" approach. This modern methodology is core. It is characterized by a consultative, customer-centric, and relationship-oriented approach that prioritizes the buyer's needs at the heart of the process. The shift reflects a change in consumer behavior, where well-informed buyers now expect salespeople to be trusted advisors who offer genuine value, rather than merely reciting product features.

"Whatever you project, it will come back to you"
Depack Chopra (Spiritual Teacher)

Different Sales Models

Different sales models include Consultative, Solution, Transactional, Inbound, and Account-Based selling. Each of these focus on distinct approaches to customer needs during the sales process. Consultative selling acts as a trusted advisor, while Solution selling identifies a specific problem. Transactional selling is a fast-paced, volume-driven approach focused on individual sales, whereas Inbound selling relies on attracting customers with valuable content. Account-Based selling targets specific high-value accounts and modules, such as challenging sales and spin selling, offering specific questioning and insight-driven frameworks for engaging customers.

Be a Visionary

Once you are assigned your clients or territory, you need to first conceptualize as a whole what you want to achieve. Once you do that task, the wheels will be put in motion for your planning stage. The more energy you put into forecasting the success of your assignments, and you put your work ethic behind it, the more results you will see from your efforts.

"We are very good at what we do, we're very professional, but we're also very creative. We can improvise. We can do things that the adversary doesn't expect."
James Taiclet (CEO of Lockheed Martin)

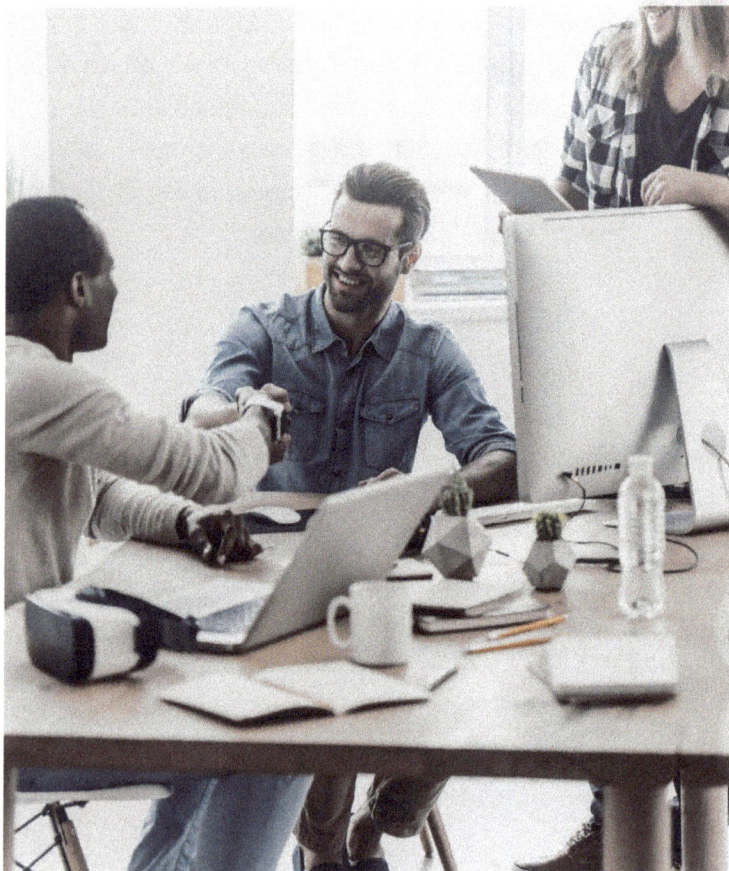

Planning

When it comes to planning, I have used several models until I settled on one that works well for me. At the beginning of my career you could say I used a bottom-up planning model that was task oriented with no real clear overall objective. After five years of doing this, I changed my focus on how I viewed my objectives. As I became more proficient as a category specialist, the more I started to move away from tasks and moved into conceptual selling. I began to view my sales territory from a broader perspective. I started to look at my sales territory from a bigger picture, and I started to plan from the top of the pyramid down, rather than managing the bottom pyramid detail-oriented tasks up that had a minimum fiscal return. It's a top-down approach and when you do this, you can look at the details of the big picture that will help you drive your business. You're not abandoning good planning; you're just shifting your paradigm to focus on greater success.

One key element in client relations that helped me sustain meaningful relationships with my clients was the ability to connect one session or call to the next. A previous employer taught me this tactic and here it is in a nutshell: you will need a pack of index cards and when you call your clients, ask about their hobbies and interests. Write each client's interest and hobbies on the index card and file them away for future reference when you call the person again. It is amazing what they will tell you and your clients will enjoy your taking an interest in their personal life. With each and every session or call with a client, take a mental note or write down on the index card about how that call ended. When you revisit that account, you can follow up with the client regarding the conversation from the previous call. I found this connectivity to be very effective in communicating and selling the benefits of my platforms to clients.

Build Flexibility Into Your Planning

When you are creating your weekly and monthly plan, it's important to incorporate flexibility into your planner to reflect the moving market that you are experiencing. All markets have fluidity and we must adapt to the marketplace. A fluid market refers to a dynamic marketplace characterized by constant evolution and unpredictability. This environment is shaped by shifts in consumer preferences, competitors' strategies, and economic conditions. Being responsive means effectively sensing and adapting to these changes when you see them. The ability to respond quickly to market shifts can provide a significant competitive advantage. Adapting to new consumer behaviors and industry trends helps maintain a competitive edge and prevents you from becoming obsolete. Swift responsiveness allows businesses to capitalize on emerging trends and new market opportunities. Recognizing organizational speed as a method to respond to the marketplace is proven tool to help your business prioritize understanding and meeting the evolving customer expectations and needs.

"You have to have a business model you believe in."
Brian L. Roberts (CEO of Comcast)

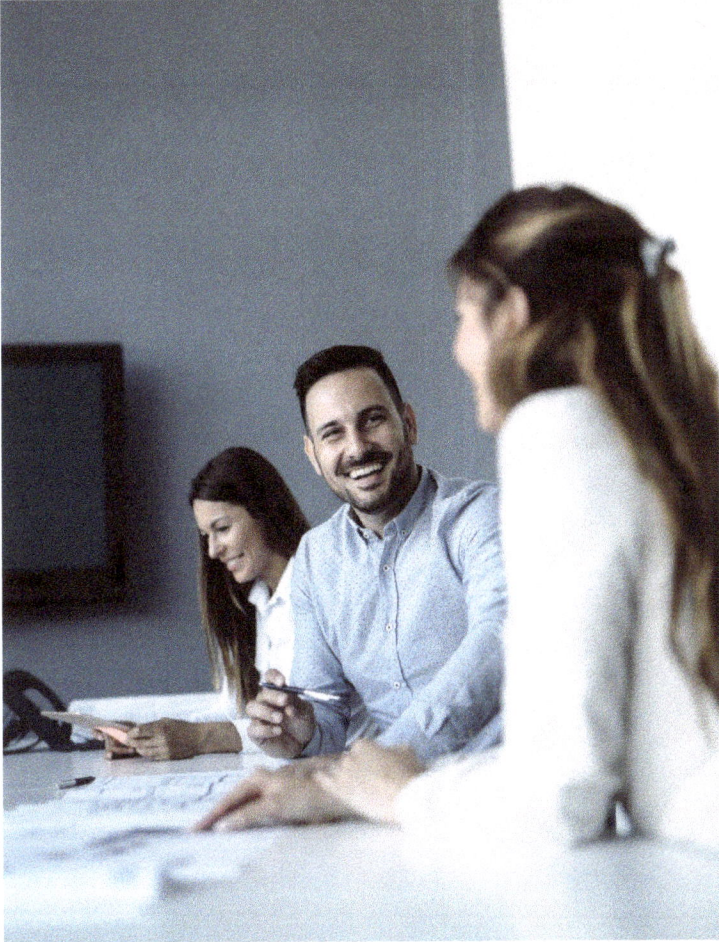

You Get What You Accept

The theory of the statement "You get what you accept" is a principle based on a universal cycle that rewards the approach that you can never become complacent in life. If you believe you will always reap rewards based on the effort you put forth, you will continue to propel forward, encountering new opportunities. With this attitude, the lens through which you view life will never be the same, since you will see things from a new perspective. Imagine viewing life as if you are on top of a mountain. You can see the path you traveled to get to your destination and see what still lies ahead. The history of where you came from plays an important role as you prepare for future endeavors. As you look at the view from the top of this metaphorical mountain, you gain clarity on how to reach your goals because you understand you are not limited in your abilities.

Throughout history, humanity has made remarkable advancements, driven by creativity, imagination, and an innate need to improve. From the invention of the wheel, the development of language, the discovery of electricity, and the creation of modern technologies, such as the cell phone, progress has been shaped by humans' ability to innovate. These achievements fundamentally transformed our world and propelled humanity forward.

At the heart of this progress is the God-given gift of human capacity—the drive, willpower, and determination that have enabled humanity to push boundaries and achieve the seemingly impossible. Over the millennia, our greatest quest has been to overcome fear and continually expand our minds and horizons.

This pursuit of growth and self-improvement remains central to unlocking our full potential and fulfilling the highest expression of ourselves.

Communication

When I was a territory sales manager, I learned to embrace the notion that I can communicate and set the wheels in motion with my accounts while I'm not with them. I would send a monthly newsletter to my clients to reinforce our company's core strategies and share my thoughts on our goals, thereby strengthening our relationship and aligning with the values of our strategy. From my experience, the monthly newsletter was very beneficial to me because when I arrived for my monthly call, my clients would ask me questions for further insight on our core strategies and for goal-setting ideas.

Being Decisive

At the beginning of my sales career, if a significant problem arose, I would always weigh the pros and cons of every issue and think, think, and ponder. I started to realize that I was vacillating too much, and then I got mad at myself for not being decisive. So, I made a commitment to be more decisive in the future and once I started to be more decisive, I realized I had more peace of mind. Yes, I still pondered the pros and cons, but not to the same degree as before. Once you are decisive, you unleash an energy that is full of certainty, and you need to not doubt your ability and second-guess yourself. However, once you unleash this energy, you are always measuring your progress for adjustments. From my experience, I have found that this attitude brings you the most peace of mind. While you are unleashing your power, you believe with total conviction that you are doing the right thing for that issue.

Words Have Power

In the seventh year of my 25-year career with a Fortune 8 consumer products company, which had its products in 32 percent of American supermarket shelves, I realized that words have power. Yes, I was giving presentations and being effective, but this was the tip of the iceberg. My dad was a great salesman. He would always say throughout my life, "Always be selling" to your clients. This meant not just making a good presentation, but rather that salesmanship is a communicable art form, and you really need to educate yourself on the language of communication. When you can say words with impact, it can really change the course of your life. There is etheric energy in your vocal cords, and it has resonating power when you speak. In many holistic traditions, this is recognized, and that's why when we fluctuate our voices during a presentation, the impact is much greater because your audience appreciates the pitch and fluctuation in your voice.

"Culture is not the priority – it is the priority"
Ron Vachris (CEO of Lockheed Martin)

Retool Presentations

The most crucial element in the presentation process is not to give up if your client does not accept your presentation the first time you give it. Instead, look back, work to understand the client's objectives, and find win-win ideas that are common ground solutions. This may require digging deeper into the content and looking at the problem from a fresh perspective. You shouldn't just look at your own needs, but consider your client's needs and solve those problems before your next presentation.

Open-Ended Questions

Open-ended questions are crucial in sales because they encourage prospects to provide detailed information, reveal their true needs, and vulnerabilities. They also help build trust and rapport by demonstrating genuine curiosity and a desire to help. This approach enables a salesperson to identify potential objections, gather information that helps them understand the client's needs, and offer customized solutions based on ideas that address those needs. Here are some examples of open-ended questions to help you set the stage with your accounts:

- Mr. Client, would extra resources help you grow your business?

- Mr. Client, how do you view your account in your community?

- Mr. Client, I have prepared a presentation for you that may grow your business in this competitive market. Can we single out a date in the near future so we can sit down and discuss it?

Open-ended questions are the lifeline to encourage the client to talk and provide information, which is critical for the sales process.

"We have to organize against outcomes, not tasks".
Marshall Ganz
(Former Professor at Harvard Kennedy School)

Conceptual Selling

A conceptual selling presentation delivers superior results by focusing on the customer's needs and vision, leading to a higher closing rate and a stronger long-term relationship. In contrast, a task-driven presentation focuses on product features and transaction steps, often resulting in lower engagement and shorter customer life cycles. With conceptual selling, you are selling ideas about your product and the equity themes associated with it. You are also laying out a course and a vision for your brands and products. Conceptual selling is a consultative sales method where the seller positions their product as the concept the buyer is looking for, not just a set of features. It emphasizes a deep understanding of the buyer's pain points and goals. I have found in my sales career that if I am focused on the concepts that are important to me and my company, as well as the long-term vision of the success of the client's business, then I am one step ahead of the competition.

Trial and Error

"Success is the sum of many things done well," said Bob Casey, the founder of UPS. Let's examine this quote more carefully. As you progress towards your objective for success, the synergy of trial and error and reflection is the most potent energy you possess to reach your objective. As you pursue life, you will encounter many obstacles. In your path, the key learning for you is not to give up and to use the lesson of reflection to look back and examine your mistakes and see where you can improve.

*"Never promise more than you can deliver, and
always deliver what you promise"*
Bob Casey (Founder of United Parcel Service)

Brevity in Selling

During my sales career, I started to realize the importance of brevity in my presentations. Brevity is crucial in presentations because it respects your audience's time, leading to greater engagement and improved credibility. Concise presentations and enhanced clarity, prevents audience fatigue, and demonstrates your mastery of the subject matter. By focusing on essential points and eliminating unnecessary words, you create a sharper, more focused delivery that increases audience attention and ensures your core message is understood and remembered with impact.

Storytelling

Telling a story while presenting is impactful because stories evoke emotion, simplify complex ideas, and foster a deeper connection between the audience and the presenter. All of which makes the presentation more memorable. A compelling narrative activates more parts of the brain and turns abstract data into concrete experiences. These things help the audience to relate, understand, and retain the message far better than merely reciting facts. Stories trigger emotional responses, helping the audience connect with the presenter on a deeper level. By focusing on the creative side of the brain, rather than the analytical side, you can look forward to a 26 percent increase in retention of information from your audience.

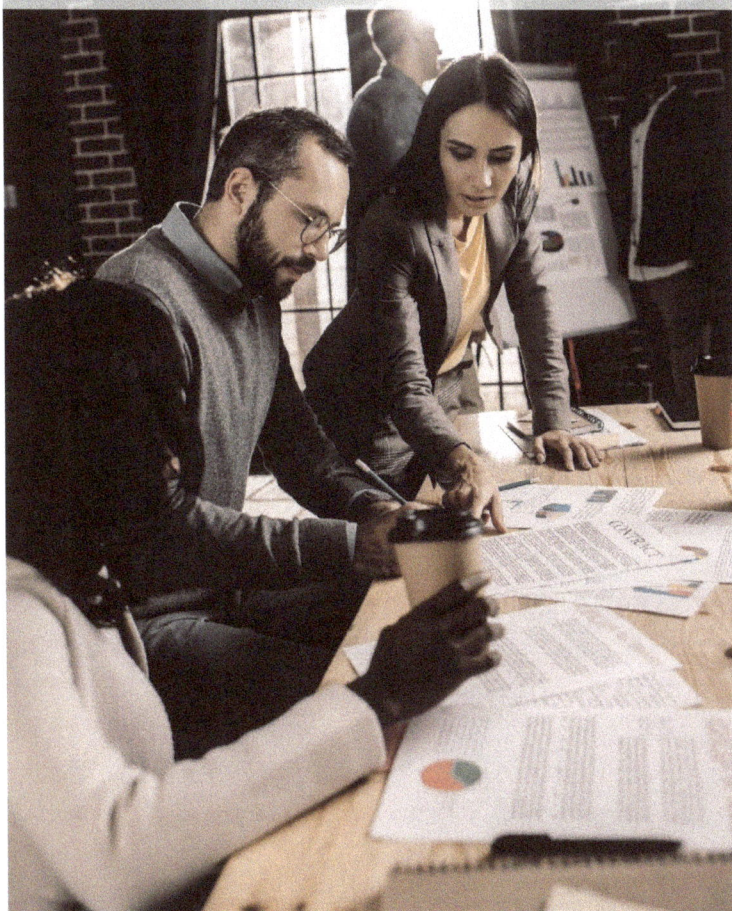

"*Self – praise is for losers. Be a winner. Stand for something. Always have class, and be humble*"
John Madden (Former Hall of Fame Coach)

The First Objection

In one of the selling books that I read to help me become a more well-rounded salesperson, a very helpful idea came from it that I would like to share with you. While engaging your client, the first objection from that person is a smokescreen, and the real objection that reflects the client's real needs are located in the second objection The first objection is a blow off to move you along without the client getting into his or her needs. When this happens in most situations, the client wants help but doesn't know who to trust with his or her needs. As a salesperson, the key for me was to have enough material to handle the first objection and save my best material for the real objection. Once I started doing this, I became a much more well-rounded salesperson.

Having Two Closing Scenarios

I have read numerous materials from multiple sources on selling techniques, and the one that had the most impact on me was having two closing scenarios. As you go through the selling process and discuss the features and benefits of your product, here is the point I would like to make. Every close is different because of the background and the needs of the account are different and that is why fact gathering is critical before every presentation. If you do your job correctly and lay out how your product can help with the client's needs, you could say, "If we're in agreement that all your needs are satisfied, can we please move forward to our vision?" (First Close)

Then, I would pull out a calendar and ask them which of the two dates was best for the product and merchandise rack to arrive at their store. Ninety-five percent of the time, they would pick one of those two dates.

By doing this, you're giving them control by allowing them to choose the dates, empowering them, which unifies trust between the client and the salesperson, and you walk out the door with the sale. (Second Close)

Solution Selling

As a Territory Sales Manager, I effectively utilized a sales process to help resolve problems that arose. It was very effective. The first thing you have to do is to identify the problem, then use open-ended questions to help flush out the client's concerns and issues. The next step is to come to a solution and agree on the client's issue. The final step is to formalize an action plan that both you and the client agree on to follow through on during your next call with the client.

Betting on Yourself

You could have the best technology, facts, and analysis, but nothing helps you more than betting on yourself to excel and exceed all your objectives. After all, when it comes down to it, you're the one who must take ownership of your destiny. The beauty of your destiny is that it always involves you until you reach and complete your objectives. Of course, life is about many destinies, constantly churning on a never-ending quest of possibilities. Even in retirement, you may take on hobbies that lead to new insights. Remember, the view is always the same, unless you're the lead dog.

"Effort equals results"
(a favorite quote from his father)
Roger Penske (Founder of Team Penske)

Boldness

Many people do not use their abstract abilities, particularly boldness, where they can change their dynamic to propel themselves forward with energy. Most people opt for a life of safety, rather than embracing boldness. When you choose boldness, you are taking a step in believing in yourself. You are empowering yourself with positive messaging to reinforce your will and sustain you as you overcome obstacles to reach your goals.

An investment of positive energy is not wasted because words come from thoughts, which have the power to transmute our intentions. One of the elements of faith is to believe in the impossible. This is an element of faith, which is believing in something greater than yourself.

Synergy

What I have observed as a Territory Sales Manager is that when you put enough energy into your sales and assignments, your production will be returned to you more than you can realize. Remember Deepak Chopra's quote, "Whatever you invest, comes back to you." Still, it's more than that. When you invest enough energy into your sales and assignments, your climate will take on a nucleus of itself, and this nucleus can drive superior results, if you continue to manage it correctly.

"Be authentic. Be yourself, and work at places that really welcome who you are".
Karen S. Lynch (Former CEO of CVS)

Believing in the Impossible

One element that I held throughout my entire selling career was the belief that anything was possible. You must believe with your whole heart and invest energy in the belief that anything can be achieved through believing in the impossible. Once you believe in this, events start to unravel for you in a positive way. Of course, you have to put the time and effort in for this to work. When you do, the dividends can be huge. You should start to feel a synergy of events, which reflects the cause-and-effect relationship in your work environment.

Life Expands from the Mind

Life expands from the mind, for it reverberates through your assignments. Positive energy sparks a wave of energy that spreads beyond the body and ripples across atmospheric frequencies, creating a wave of positive motion that helps promote and influence your assignments and global consciousness.

Some people say that life is not fair, but if you work hard and live a life of boldness and courage, you can turn the tides of life in your favor. John Milton once said, "Luck is the residue of design." Life expands and contracts like a rubber band. The key to success is to sacrifice and apply yourself. By doing those things, you'll stay on top of the hill, more than the valley.

"Sing, boy! sing! The ages are waiting for you. Sing! sing! All the world will hear you. God knows what will come of it."
Charles Coffin (Famous Hymn Composer)

Settling

Comfort is a significant danger in sales, as it leads to stagnation, decreased productivity, and missed growth opportunities.

By avoiding complacency and embracing discomfort, salespeople can achieve greater long-term success and become top performers. Resting on past success, like a high-earning account, creates a comfort zone that prevents you from seeking new clients or improving your skills. This leads to a slow decline that competitors, who are constantly pushing their boundaries, will quickly exploit. You must set a standard of excellence for yourself and consistently seek to self-evaluate to see if you are settling. Don't settle. Instead, chart a new path forward to challenge the status quo.

Positive Frame of Mind

It is essential to apply discipline to your daily life and to maintain a positive frame of mind. Every thought releases some type of chemical. When you work at staying positive, and positive thoughts are being generated, you typically feel happy and optimistic. This is because endorphins are released, cortisol levels decrease, and serotonin production increases. When serotonin levels are normal, it helps us to feel happy, calmer, less anxious, and more emotionally stable.

Let's look at the prefrontal cortex of the brain. When happy thoughts occur, there is brain growth in the frontal lobe. This happens as a result of the reinforcement of thousands of neurons being fired in the frontal lobe..

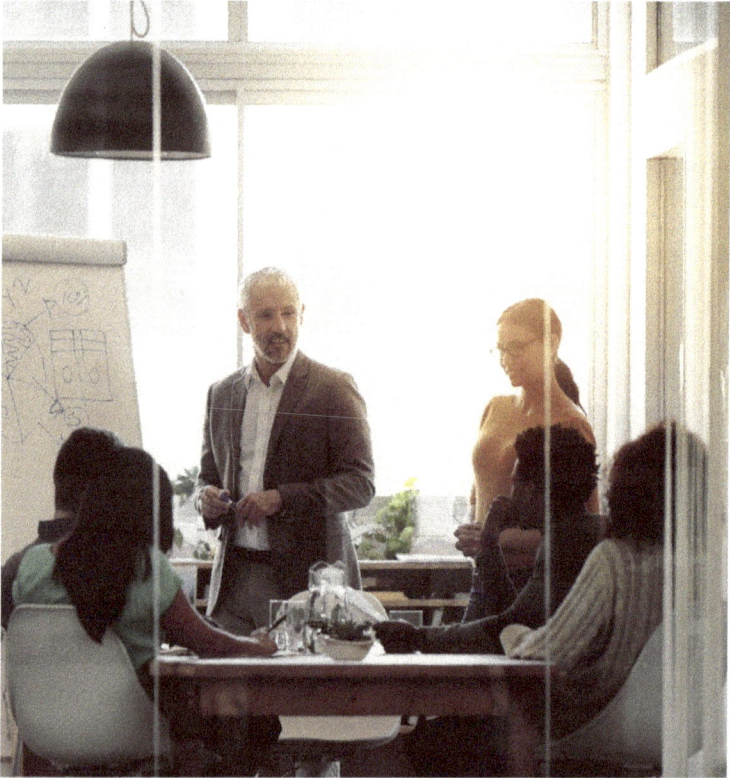

"The desire to fly is an idea handed down to us by our ancestors who, in their grueling travels across trackless lands in prehistoric times, looked enviously on the birds soaring freely through."
Sam Walton

The brain is essential for unleashing the power of your mind. When you release the power of your mind, there are no limits to the size and scope of what can come into your life. The scope of the material world is immeasurable in relation to your spirit and what you can achieve when you believe. Nothing is impossible for you! The point is to embrace life because life in itself is inexhaustible in its opportunities. If you took that fragment and applied to your capabilities in your assignment, it is endless what you can achieve.

The Meaning of Resilience

Resilience in desperate times is a powerful force that enhances our instincts to get up and try again.

As the great writer Emerson teaches, "Whilst he sits on the cushion of advantages, he goes to sleep. When he is pushed, tormented, he has a chance to learn something." Being game for your own challenges, realizing you're equal to the tasks that life sets before you, is enormously empowering.

Knowledge is the antidote to fear. It's so important to look at life with a positive outlook. It's something to work at, but the dividends are enormous and very impactful in our lives. When setbacks occur, it is essential to find a way to overcome them in order to find value in the things you do. Setbacks are learning opportunities that enable a person to become more well-rounded.

Forward-thinking action helps us strengthen our minds by enabling the brain to change and grow in response to life experiences. For this to happen, a person must adopt a positive attitude towards life.

"A people who are possessed of the spirit of commerce, who see and who will pursue their advantages may achieve almost anything."
George Washington (Founding Father)

Whenever a person takes a decisive move forward because it is felt deeply in the heart and soul, that person is emboldened by energy that supports a definitive position.

Resilience is not a trait people either have or don't have. Gaining resilience involves behaviors, thoughts, and actions that can be learned and developed by everyone.

Over Analysis Causes Paralysis

I read in Fortune Magazine many years ago that it is essential to keep the decision-making process as close as possible to the point of execution. This can only be achieved when you think you are a category expert, which we discussed earlier in this book. When you are close to the execution point of decision-making and you have a subjective decision to make, in most cases, you would need to go up the chain of command in a company to get approval to go forward. I have learned from past experience that you can't depend on your immediate manager or supervisor to make the best decision for you, even though you have presented the best argument for what you want to be approved. Sadly, office politics always seem to be the case in these types of scenarios, as the manager will usually side with caution and dampen your instincts. If you look at the most successful people in history, you will see that they were risk-takers. This is where you come in, assuming you are a category specialist and you are the closest to the decision-making process. When you know all the pros and cons of the situation, and you have to make a decision, do it based on your instincts that your vision will prevail down the road. Of

"The day will come when the man on the telephone will be able to see the other person at the other end of the telephone."
Alexander Grapham Bell (Inventor of the telephone)

course, with every risk comes responsibility you have to take upon yourself, and that's a burden that all risk takers have to live with, but the payoff can be significant, if your hunches are correct.

True North

In a spiritual context, "True North" represents a fixed, unwavering point of guidance, often symbolizing a person's highest values, core beliefs, or a divine source that acts as an internal compass.

One's "True North" guides a person through life's decisions and challenges, much like the North Star guided navigators of old. It is a constant reference point, helping one stay aligned with their authentic self and purpose, even when faced with external distractions or conflicting opinions.

A key point about "True North" is spirituality or your inner compass.

Inner compass: "True North" is often described as an internal compass, meaning it's not an external concept, rather a deeply held understanding of what is right and true for the individual.

It's essential to undertake a self-analysis of your strengths and weaknesses and formulate a plan with prayer and guidance as you partake in this journey to move forward in your life.

Being Passionate

The first core of being passionate is having the right attitude: loving life with all its blessings every day. If you do that, you see the world differently.

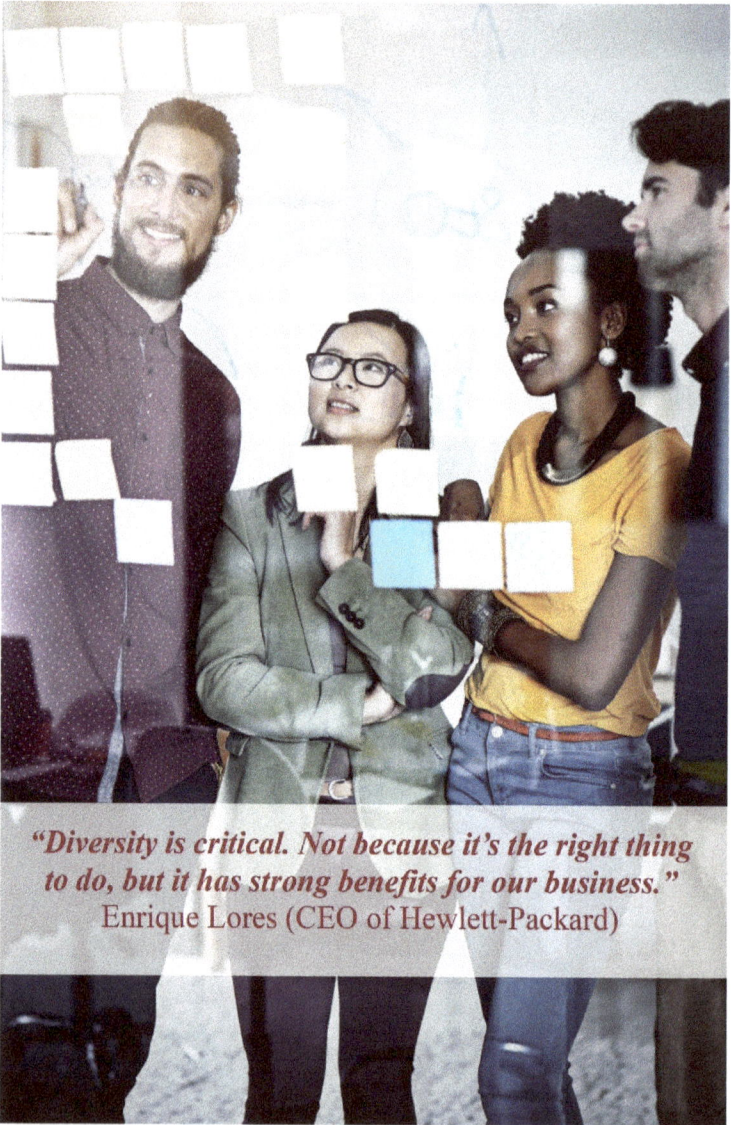

"*Diversity is critical. Not because it's the right thing to do, but it has strong benefits for our business.*"
Enrique Lores (CEO of Hewlett-Packard)

This is important because this is the core of where you get your passion and happiness from. Once you understand who you are and what makes you tick, you need to align those values with the right job for you. That doesn't mean you don't apply yourself to everything you do, but there is a difference between working hard and being passionate. Passion is a powerful and compelling emotion characterized by strong feelings, intense enthusiasm, and deep devotion towards something. You find this when you follow your instincts and your "True North". Whatever you invest in will come back to you, many times over, but you must put in the time and work. Nothing will be given to you.

Connectivity

The way to extract the maximum return from a problem is to look at it from the inside out. For example, if an engine is compromised, sugarcoating the problem without finding a solution will just result in a patch-up job with a minimum return.

To maximize your return, you'll need to address the core issues to bring them into harmony and have better connectivity and efficiency. This will enable you to flourish as you continue down the path towards achieving your goals.

Every job doesn't have the same opportunity to incorporate this approach of co-creation. If you aren't as fortunate, many hobbies can utilize your imagination. When your spirit combines with imagination, the impact on yourself is bountiful.

Before you do anything, you need to plan. You need to identify and evaluate your problems. It helps if your beliefs are anchored in faith because your faith will always support a foundation of free-flowing love in all your endeavors.

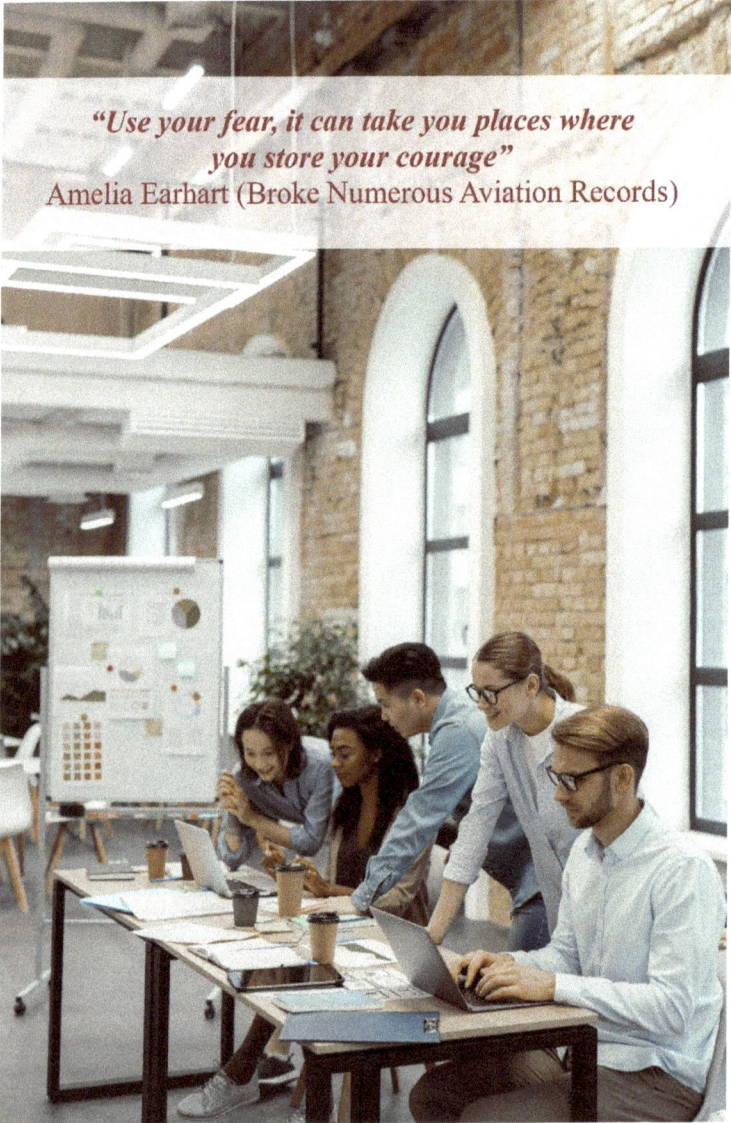

"Use your fear, it can take you places where you store your courage"
Amelia Earhart (Broke Numerous Aviation Records)

The key is to invest your energy so that you'll live a purposeful life. An intentional life is one that's guided by values and passions, and those things positively contribute to the world. It involves finding meaning and satisfaction in your life, as well as being dedicated to growing and learning.

Manifestation – Can Optimism Change Reality?

Findings from a 2007 study conducted by neuroscientist Elizabeth Phelps suggests that a region in the frontal cortex of the brain is responsible for directing feelings of optimism in our brain.

Mind propulsion is necessary to create a state of believing that the mind is infinite. The mind can explore the borders of our imagination. God is bountiful and is beyond all boundaries, and so is the potential of all humanity to live a life of limitless awareness. We are capable of moving mountains, and nothing is impossible for you.

Expectations become self-fulfilling prophecies by altering our performance and actions, which ultimately affect what happens in the future.

Materialization in the physical world occurs when the deep regions in your brain receive your positive thoughts and intentions from the cortex and then transmit this information out into the universe, which understands all your needs. Mind propulsion is necessary to propel the mind forward to do this.

The brain is made up of the same atoms and molecules that are in the rest of the universe. A new study found similarities between

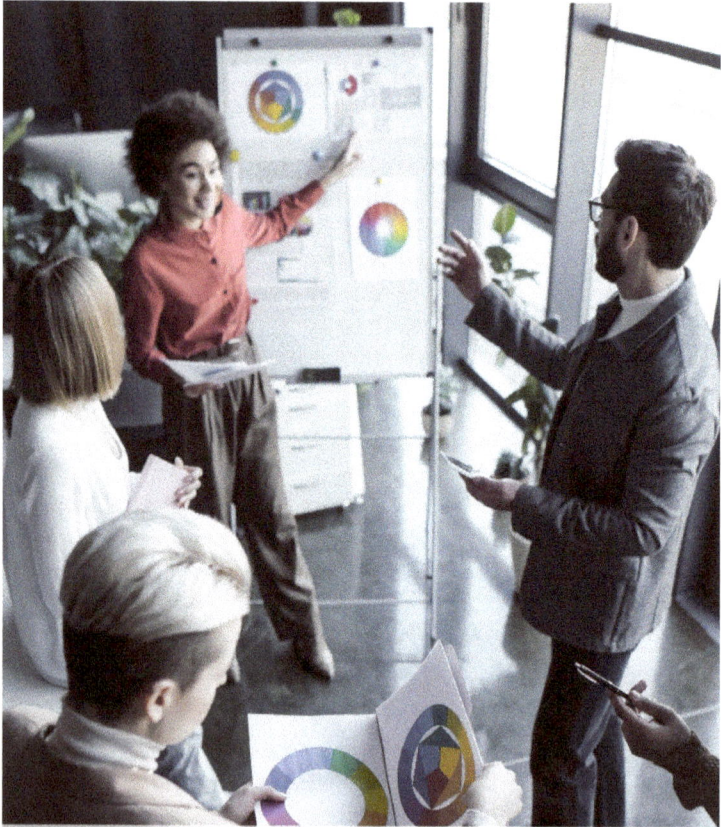

"In times of great stress or adversity, it's always best to keep busy, to plow your anger and your energy into something positive"
Lee Iacocca (Former President of Ford)

the human brain and the network of galaxies. When the universe receives your positive thoughts, it puts into motion the wheels to bring your thoughts into materialization. (contributing material from Time Magazine).

Illustration of Universal Brain

The illustration below indicates that when you work hard and generate positive thoughts, the thoughts get transmitted out to the universe, which understands all your needs. The universe, which has a similar galactic cerebral shape, will help put the wheels in motion to bring things into fruition in your life. (Time Magazine)

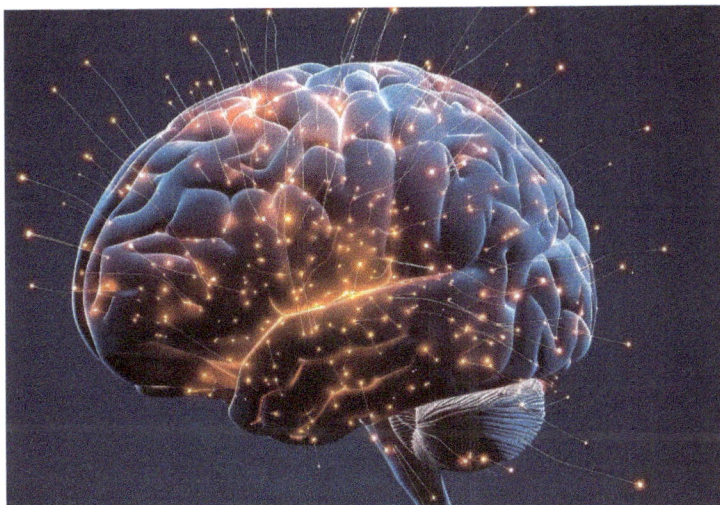

Simplicity and Execution

If you followed every rule and procedure laid out by your company, you would probably dilute the execution process between you and the end result. Your company uses all kinds of rules and guidelines as safeguards to create an environment of checks and balances that ensures complicity. You must think creatively to help yourself increase the product execution between you and the end result. Every company has its rules and regulations. These rules are necessary because they provide guidance for their employees. Of course, that doesn't mean we can't enhance those rules and regulations. If you choose to be creative and start enhancing on top of your company's rules, please weigh all the pros and cons and calculate the risk options for yourself before doing anything. Find out if your company encourages risk. Some organizations promote risk because they believe it is beneficial to the organization. If you have a good idea, carefully consider it, within the scope of your company's rules and regulations, and think it will work, that's something to consider. While I benefited greatly from risk-taking, it is a decision you must make for yourself.

The Universe Is Within Us

The universe was created so that all motion has a cause and an effect outcome. This means that the output of all energy has a positive or negative impact, which can affect your life. It all starts with intention. When your intentions are good, you can improve your outcomes, which can lead to greater materialization.

"All our dreams can come true if we have the courage to pursue them."
Walt Disney

What makes up the universe is also represented in us. The electrons, protons, and atoms that exist in the universe also exist in us. By learning to understand the forces within us, we can enhance our own well-being.

The universe is a powerful ally in bringing concepts, ideas, and plans to fruition. Understanding the components and how the universe works can help you achieve all your goals.

Remember, the way to align yourself with the universe is to meditate or contemplate the meaning of your awareness, as you understand it. By doing this, you will align a connection with the universe, which is very powerful for assisting with all your goals. Once you have implemented your action plan, it's essential to cross the threshold from thought to execution.

It's essential to let love lead the way with your best intentions. When you set a path of unconditional intentions with no entitlements, you are embarking on a path of freedom, which is unbridled beyond your imagination, to bridge the gap between greatness and your own self-limited beliefs.

Value Added Services

Value-added services are critical to any sales position because they show the customer that you care about them, which can go a long way toward the longevity of the sale. Value-added services come in a variety of packages, but they typically focus on solving customers' problems, providing convenience, or offering unique problem-solving experiences, moving beyond the product itself. I can recall one time when one of my accounts got in one of my large merchandising fixtures, which required a lot of cardboard

"The biggest adventure you can ever take is to live the life of your dreams," "Turn your wounds into wisdom," and "Think like a queen. A queen is not afraid to fail. Failure is another steppingstone to greatness".
Oprah Winfrey

wrapping, which consumed much of his dumpster in his parking lot. I went out to assess the situation and realized that the only way to help my client with his needs was to climb into the dumpster and break down the cardboard by hand with my razor to his satisfaction. When I returned, he had already agreed to bring in the maximum amount allowed for a new brand. He was so thankful for the value-added service that he told me that he owned four other accounts in my assignment that I just took over, and my company is welcome in all his accounts with his support for all future promotions. This is an excellent example of the positive intangibles of value-added services.

Let the Buyer Make the Decision

There are some instances during the selling process when you can allow the buyer to come to the conclusion that he is making the decision about the outcome of the sales presentation. This requires listening to the talking points between you and the buyer. If you are presenting and the buyer is nodding his head and giving you favorable gestures, then you should change course in your presentation and say something like this, " Mr. Buyer, we seem to be in agreement on many of the key talking points, do you have any thoughts that would contribute to bringing this plan into fruition?" If all the talking points and body gestures were favorable during the presentation, your buyer will often surprise you and give you the green light to write the order. If he has further questions, you're allowing the buyer to participate in the selling process, and isolating his final objectives to wrapping up the deal.

"The biggest risk is not taking any risk... In a world that changing really quickly, the only strategy that is guaranteed to fail is not taking risks."
Mark Zuckerburg   (Founder and CEO of Facebook)

Fact Gathering

Before every presentation, it is critical that you cross all the T's, dot all the I's, and do all the necessary fact gathering on that account before the start of any presentation. This is necessary because, as the buyer raises objections, a well-prepared sales manager should have done the necessary fact-gathering on the buyer's needs to overcome them.

Suggestive Selling

Suggestive Selling is a sales technique in which the seller recommends additional complementary products or services to a customer to enhance their original purchase, increasing the sale's value and improving the customer experience by meeting unstated needs. Typical examples include extending the warranty with electronics and telling the client you have a reputation for providing high-quality service. Suggestive Selling often adds value to the sales call and gives you an opportunity to sell yourself because you're not just selling a service or a product. People often forget that the client must believe in the salesperson before they are ever sold anything, so the first thing you must sell is yourself.

Talking Points

It is so important to do your homework and study all the trade journals in your profession, so you can have talking points for your clients ready. This will show your clients that you have taken the time to understand their business, which will gain their respect because you want them think of you as a category expert. Once they do that, your relationship moves towards a more trusting relationship. The end game is that you will have more sales because you put the time in to study.

Overcome Objections

As you are coming to the end of the sales presentation and you've covered all your features and benefits of your product, and you don't want to answer an endless number of objections from your client, you can say, "Mr. Client, do you have any concerns that you would like to bring to my attention before we proceed?" And once he mentions his objections, you should say, "Mr. Client, are these the only objections that you can think of?" This question isolates his concerns and quantifies them, so you, as a well-prepared sales manager, can overcome them.

The reason this is so important is if you don't isolate his questions, you will allow him to continue to run off objections and ponder new ones while he is thinking. Quantifying him and letting him provide you with his upfront concerns gives you an opportunity to overcome them and close the deal by saying, "With your permission, let's move forward with this business plan to put your account in the best opportunity to grow incremental business."

"If everyone is moving forward together, then success takes care itself."
Henry Ford (Founder of Ford Motor Company)

Assuming the Sale

Let's assume you're calling on an account in your assignment and you've done all your footwork and fact gathering and you want to Assume the Sale and to close the deal. Somewhere along the sales process you should say something like this, "After looking at all the evidence of your account, are we in agreement that you would like your account to be more competitive in your category"? This will certainly get an affirmation from your client. Once you have that commitment, then you can proceed with Assuming the Sale method, where you say, "If we agree with all the principles in this presentation, let's move forward with our goal in mind to position you as a market leader in your community, which you said was a goal of yours."

Concepts Drive the Business

Concepts drive the business through brand equity, which builds value with customers. When you combine concepts with messaging, the impact can be significant, especially when the product is of high quality. Customers are always looking for value and quality, and you can sell an item that could be a premium brand. Yet, consumers perceive many values in the brand for its quality, like Tide detergent, which is consistently the best-selling laundry detergent nationwide. This brand gets its message out on television, creating loyalty with its customer base while maintaining its great quality, creating value with its brand equity. Another brand that is also number one in sales is Hellmann's

Mayonnaise, which connects with its customers with its slogan "Bring out the Hellmann's, bring out the best."

Another product that customers have believed in because of its messaging and quality, is Marlboro cigarettes. Despite how you feel about tobacco, it is one of the biggest turnarounds and concept drivers among advertised products. In 1954 it was positioned as a woman's cigarette and sales were flat. Then, in late 1954, Leo Burnett's ad agency was hired by Philip Morris to reposition the Marlboro brand, introducing the slogan "Come to where the flavor is, come to Marlboro Country" and launching the cowboy theme. The campaign transformed Marlboro into a best-selling brand by the 1960s. My point is that concepts drive the business, but you need people to implement the values of your company's mission statement and your products, which are also concepts.

Knowledge is Power

As I have mentioned throughout this book, I advise you to seek out and absorb as much information as possible from all the various sources related to your job, including your competition. When you do this on a daily basis, you will start to coalesce and assimilate your information and be able to articulate it in a fluid delivery.

When you can combine this cohesion of information from the various sources within your presentation, it will be so much more effective and communicate your point with impact to your client. As a result, the client will look upon you more as an expert in your field, which builds more value with your client.

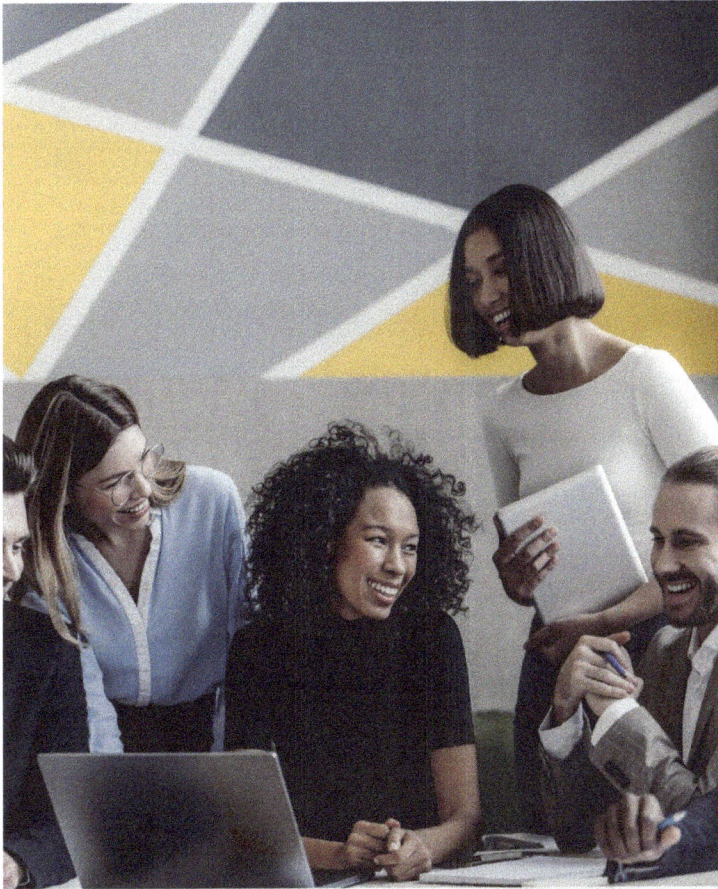

"Success is a lousy teacher. It seduces smart people into thinking they can't lose," "Life is not fair; get used to it," "The best way to prepare is to write programs, and to study great programs that other people have written".
Bill Gates (Founder of Microsoft)

Labor of Love

You have to want it! You have to be hungry for it! Even if you become successful, winners strive to win, despite their accolades. From this essence, everything unravels, because this is the core of all good things that will evolve in your life. As you unearth your hidden talents, due to your persistence, you will continue to evolve, because this is your natural course. All of this is born from your labor of love.

Recommended Selling Books for Your Reading Pleasure

1. "Everyone Lives by Selling Something," an essay in the book *Across the Plains* by Robert Louis Stevenson

This 19th-century author's observation is often cited for its profound insight into the ubiquity of selling.

Key takeaway: The essay argues that "selling" is not a profession limited to salesmen but a fundamental aspect of all human interaction. Lawyers sell their arguments, doctors sell their expertise, and politicians sell their ideas. Recognizing this broader truth reframes selling as a core life skill rather than a disreputable practice.

2. *The Philosophy of a Sale* by Robert P. DeGraff

This text expands on the idea that selling is not about coercion but about service and finding the right solution for a client.

Key takeaway: DeGraff's work emphasizes that long-term relationships and customer satisfaction are the proper measures of success. It promotes a sales philosophy based on integrity, trust, and a focus on the customer's best interest.

3. *To Sell Is Human* by Daniel H. Pink

Pink's work is a modern classic that offers a profound reframing of selling for the 21st century.

Key takeaway: Pink argues that in a world of readily available information, the old model of the salesperson as an information gatekeeper is obsolete. Modern selling is about attunement, buoyancy (resilience), and clarity. He shows how these principles are essential not just in traditional sales but in almost every profession.

4. "The Art of the Start 2.0" by Guy Kawasaki

This book contains an influential chapter on pitching and evangelism.

Key takeaway: Kawasaki's core idea is that the best way to sell an idea is to become an evangelist for it. This means focusing on passion and genuine belief rather than high-pressure tactics. He also emphasizes that the best pitches are not about closing a deal but about creating a vision that people want to be a part of.

Essays on the ethics and philosophy of selling

5. "Why You Need a Selling Philosophy" by Prudent Pedal

This online essay argues for developing a personal "selling philosophy" grounded in values.

Key takeaway: The author emphasizes the principle of "always give before you take" and helping prospects make the best decision for themselves, even if it means directing them to a competitor. This approach prioritizes building relationships over making a quick sale.

6. "Using Personal Story to Sell" by Ann Sheybani

Available on *Medium*, this essay explores the power of authenticity in selling.

Key takeaway: It critiques the corporate habit of projecting an impenetrable, superhuman image. By sharing personal stories and being more vulnerable, sellers can build a genuine connection with potential clients that is far more effective than a polished, impersonal presentation.

7. "Everyone is in Sales" by Andy Paul

Drawing on insights from his book *Sell Without Selling Out*, this essay and others by Paul challenge the traditional sales mindset.

Key takeaway: Paul's work argues that relationships and trust are the primary drivers of purchase decisions. He insists that sellers must focus on building authentic connections by understanding and serving their clients' needs, rather than relying on outdated, high-pressure tactics.